I'm Afraid of Spiders

But I'm Getting Treatment

Copyright © Welness Edition

Tous droits réservés.

Code ISBN : 9798340203601

Table of Contents

INTRODUCTION 7
Chapter 1: Recognizing the Fear 15
Chapter 2: Understanding Strategic Brief Therapy. 23
Chapter 3: Preparing for Change Mentally 32
Chapter 4: Confrontation Strategies 41
Chapter 5: Modifying Internal Dialogue 49
Chapter 6: Paradoxical Tasks 57
Chapter 7: Strengthening Resilience 65
Chapter 8: Living Without Fear 73
Conclusion 80

INTRODUCTION

Understanding Arachnophobia: The Fear of Spiders

Arachnophobia, or the fear of spiders, is one of the most common specific phobias worldwide. It is characterized by an intense, often irrational fear triggered by the sight, thought, or even the mention of spiders. This fear can vary in intensity from one person to another, ranging from slight disgust to a paralyzing fear that significantly impacts an individual's quality of life.

Evolutionary Origins :

To understand arachnophobia, it is essential to consider its origins. Some theories suggest that the fear of spiders is rooted in our evolution, an instinctive response developed by our ancestors for survival. In an environment where encounters with potentially dangerous animals were frequent, a fear of spiders could have served as a defense mechanism to avoid venomous bites.

Psychological Aspects :

From a psychological viewpoint, arachnophobia can be influenced by a variety of factors. Traumatic experiences related to spiders, particularly those occurring during childhood, often play a key role in the development of this fear. Additionally, observational learning, such as seeing a parent or close relative react with fear to a spider, can also contribute to adopting this phobia.

Impact on Daily Life :

The impact of arachnophobia on daily life should not be underestimated. For some people, this fear can limit their ability to participate in outdoor activities, affect their choice of housing, or even disrupt simple household tasks like cleaning. In extreme cases, the mere idea of encountering a spider can cause anxiety, panic attacks, or a total avoidance of certain situations, to the extent that one might not even go down to their cellar to fetch a good bottle of wine.

Perception and Reality :

It is important to note that the fear of spiders is not always based on a realistic assessment of the danger they pose. The vast majority of spiders are harmless to humans and, in fact, play a crucial ecological role in controlling insect populations. However, for a person suffering from arachnophobia, this knowledge is not enough to alleviate the fear.

Treatment and Overcoming :

Fortunately, arachnophobia, like other specific phobias, can be effectively treated through various therapeutic approaches. Cognitive-behavioral therapies, which involve gradual exposure to the object of fear in a controlled setting, have shown great effectiveness. Interventions can also include relaxation techniques, cognitive restructuring to change the perception of spiders, and more recent approaches like virtual reality therapy.

The Objective of This Book :

This guide is designed to accompany you on your journey towards understanding and, ultimately, overcoming your fear of spiders. By adopting a progressive approach, inspired by the work of Richard Nardone and Allen Carr's method, we will explore together practical strategies and exercises that will help you change your relationship with spiders. From recognizing and accepting your fear to controlled exposure and reassessment of your beliefs, this book aims to provide you with the tools necessary to live free from arachnophobia.

Together, we will discover that your fear, as powerful as it may be, does not define who you are. It can be understood, managed, and ultimately reduced until it is no longer a hindrance in your life. This is a path to freedom, and this guide is here to lead you through it, step by step.

Why a Step-by-Step Guide?

The Effectiveness of a Progressive Approach

The road to healing and overcoming our fears is often fraught with uncertainties and challenges. Arachnophobia, this visceral and often paralyzing fear of spiders, is no exception. Yet, why opt for a step-by-step guide to tackle such fear? The answer lies in the power and effectiveness of a progressive approach, a method that has proven its worth not only in treating phobias but also in achieving lasting and significant changes in many aspects of human life.

The Nature of Learning and Change

Learning and change do not happen overnight. They require time, patience, and, above all, a methodical progression. When we confront our fears, particularly fears as deeply rooted as arachnophobia, the shock of total immersion can often be counterproductive or even traumatic. A step-by-step guide, on the other hand, allows for a gentle and gradual acclimatization to the source of our fear, facilitating a more natural and less intimidating learning process.

The Importance of Celebrating Small Victories

Each step taken in a progressive guide is a victory in itself. These small victories play a crucial role in boosting self-confidence and motivation to continue on the path to healing. By recognizing and celebrating each progress, no matter how small, we reinforce our belief in our ability to overcome our fears. This sense of accomplishment is essential for maintaining long-term commitment to the healing process.

Personalizing the Journey

A step-by-step guide also offers the flexibility needed to tailor the healing journey to the individual. Recognizing that each person is unique, with their own experiences, levels of anxiety tolerance, and personal goals, a progressive guide allows everyone to progress at their own pace. This personalized approach ensures that the path to overcoming arachnophobia is both realistic and respectful of individual limits, thus increasing the chances of long-term success.

Evidence-Based Foundation

Progressive approaches, such as graded exposure used in cognitive-behavioral therapy, are based on solid evidence demonstrating their effectiveness in treating phobias. By breaking down the healing process into manageable steps, individuals are less likely to feel overwhelmed and more capable of managing their anxiety at each stage of the process. This method not only helps overcome the fear of spiders but also develops anxiety management skills that can be applied in other areas of life. Thus, opting for a step-by-step guide to overcome arachnophobia is a choice that relies on a deep understanding of human nature, the learning process, and change. It acknowledges the need for gentle progression, celebrates each small step forward, and offers a structure that can be adapted to the individual, all while resting on a solid scientific foundation. By embarking on this progressive journey, you give yourself the best chance of success, armed with patience, perseverance, and a proven strategy to finally live free from the fear of spiders.

Brief Introduction to Strategic Brief Therapy and Allen Carr's Method

In the world of psychotherapy and personal development, two approaches have revolutionized how we tackle change and healing: Strategic Brief Therapy, particularly that practiced at the Palo Alto school, and Allen Carr's method for quitting smoking. Although they come from different fields, these two methods share a common philosophy centered on practical solutions, effectiveness, and the speed of change. Exploring these approaches offers unique perspectives for those looking to overcome arachnophobia.

Strategic Brief Therapy: Origins and Principles

Strategic Brief Therapy, developed within the Palo Alto school context, builds on the work of therapists and researchers like Richard Nardone. This approach is distinguished by its focus on the interactions and communication patterns that sustain a problem. Rather than dwelling on the deep-seated causes or history of the problem, it aims to identify and modify the behavioral and cognitive strategies that perpetuate the problematic situation.

A key feature of this therapy is the use of paradoxical tasks and symptom prescriptions, designed to break the cycle of problematic behaviors and thoughts. By confronting the client with the absurdity or inefficacy of their usual solutions, Strategic Brief Therapy encourages rapid and often surprising changes in perception and approach to the problem.

Allen Carr's Method: A Revolution in Smoking Cessation

Allen Carr, a former accountant turned smoking cessation expert, developed a method that has helped millions to quit smoking. His philosophy is based on understanding the underlying reasons why people continue to smoke and dismantling the beliefs that support their addiction. Unlike traditional methods that focus on willpower and fighting the desire to smoke, Allen Carr's method aims to eliminate the desire to smoke itself.

The process focuses on clarifying the myths surrounding smoking, replacing the fear of quitting with a positive outlook on becoming a non-smoker. This approach frees individuals from the sensation of deprivation and transforms quitting smoking into a positive and liberating experience.

Convergence of Philosophies: Towards a Guide to Overcome Arachnophobia

By combining the philosophy of Strategic Brief Therapy with Allen Carr's method, this guide aims to offer an innovative approach to overcoming arachnophobia. The goal is to change the way individuals perceive and interact with their fear of spiders, replacing unsuccessful strategies and limiting beliefs with actions and thoughts that promote well-being and freedom.

This journey, inspired by these two approaches, is not a battle against fear, but rather a process of revelation and transformation. It invites a change in perspective, the discovery of practical strategies to deconstruct fear, and a step-by-step progression towards freedom. By tackling arachnophobia with these tools, we can pave the way for rapid and lasting healing, based on a deep understanding of oneself and a strategic approach to change.

Chapter 1: Recognizing the Fear

Identifying Your Specific Spider-Related Fears

The first step in overcoming arachnophobia, or any phobia for that matter, is to recognize and precisely identify the nature of your fear. This may seem simple on the surface, but the fear of spiders is often more complex and nuanced than it appears. It can take various forms and intensities, affecting everyone differently. By exploring and understanding your specific fears related to spiders, you lay the first stone on the path to healing.

The Multifaceted Nature of Arachnophobia

Arachnophobia is not limited to a uniform reaction of fear or disgust towards all spiders. For some, the fear may be triggered by specific aspects of spiders, such as their appearance, the way they move, or even the idea that they might be present unseen. Others may experience a more generalized fear, including everything associated with spiders, such as webs or places where they are likely to hide.

Identifying Your Triggers

The first step in identifying your specific fears is to recognize your triggers. Start by observing your reactions in the presence of spiders or when you think about them. What triggers the strongest reaction? Is it their appearance? Their speed? Their ability to appear suddenly? By understanding what specifically triggers your fear, you can begin to work in a targeted way to defuse it.

Reflection and the Fear Journal

Keeping a fear journal can be an extremely useful tool in this process. Each time you encounter a spider or find yourself thinking about them, note what happened, how you reacted, and what you think triggered that reaction. Over time, this journal can reveal patterns in your fears and help you better understand them.

Distinguishing Between Fear and Disgust

It is also important to distinguish between fear and disgust. While some may actually fear the danger or perceived threat of spiders, others may primarily feel disgust or aversion towards their appearance or behavior. This distinction is crucial as it guides how you will approach desensitization and managing your phobia.

Analyzing Underlying Beliefs

At the heart of arachnophobia often lie underlying beliefs about spiders and the danger they represent. For example, some people believe that all spiders are venomous and potentially deadly, a notion that is far from reality. By examining and challenging these beliefs, you can begin to reduce the grip of fear on you.

Towards a More Nuanced Understanding

Understanding your specific fears related to spiders is a process that requires time and introspection. It involves observing your reactions, reflecting on your beliefs, and being honest with yourself about what you truly feel. This foundational work is essential for moving towards desensitization and ultimately overcoming arachnophobia.

Recognizing and identifying your specific fears is the first crucial step in overcoming arachnophobia. By understanding what triggers your fear, distinguishing fear from disgust, and examining the underlying beliefs that fuel this fear, you prepare yourself for a more targeted and effective healing journey. This chapter aims to guide you in this initial exploration, laying the groundwork for the subsequent steps of your journey towards freedom from the fear of spiders.

Understanding the Origins of Arachnophobia

Arachnophobia, like any phobia, is a complex web of causes and influences, ranging from biological evolution to social learning. To unravel this web, it is crucial to delve into the possible origins of this visceral fear of spiders. In doing so, we open the door to a deeper understanding of ourselves and the underlying mechanisms that fuel our phobia.

Evolutionary Roots

A widely accepted theory suggests that arachnophobia has evolutionary roots. Our ancestors, living in environments where threats were omnipresent, would have benefited from an instinctive mistrust of spiders, among other creatures. These small creatures, although mostly harmless to humans, could be associated in the mind with potential threats, such as venom. This instinctive fear would then be passed down through generations, deeply embedding itself in our collective psyche.

Cultural and Social Influences

Beyond instinct, arachnophobia is also fueled by cultural and social influences. Media, tales, and myths often abound with negative portrayals of spiders, depicting them as evil, dangerous, or supernatural. These stereotypes can reinforce or create fears among individuals, even in the absence of direct negative experiences with spiders.

Learning Through Experience

Personal experiences play a significant role in the development of arachnophobia. A traumatic encounter with a spider during childhood, for example, can leave a lasting imprint, transforming a normal fear reaction into a persistent phobia. Similarly, observing a close person's fearful reaction to a spider can instill a similar reaction, even without a direct negative experience.

Recognition of Fear as a Signal

In exploring the origins of arachnophobia, it becomes clear that our fear of spiders is not just an isolated reaction, but rather a signal, a symptom of deeper mechanisms at work. Whether this fear is rooted in our DNA, shaped by our culture, or learned through our experiences, it holds keys to our understanding of the phobia and, by extension, of ourselves. By unveiling these origins, we are not seeking to eradicate fear, but rather to understand it, tame it, and learn to live with it. It is by recognizing and accepting where our fear comes from that we can begin to chart a path towards a healthier, less fear-dominated relationship with spiders. This journey of discovery and understanding is the first step towards freedom.

Exercise: Keeping a Fear Journal

Exploring arachnophobia leads us to a fundamental exercise: keeping a fear journal. This powerful tool helps you map the often unknown territory of your phobia, offering valuable insights and opportunities for personal growth. Here's how to transform your observations into a stepping stone towards overcoming the fear of spiders.

Setting Up Your Journal

Choose a notebook or a digital document that inspires confidence and tranquility. This will be the receptacle for your thoughts, fears, and progress. Decorate it if it helps you take ownership of this journal, making the exercise not only useful but also enjoyable.

Recording Experiences

Whenever you feel fear or anxiety related to spiders, take a moment to jot down the experience. Describe the situation in as much detail as possible:

Where were you?

What were you doing?

What triggered your fear?

On a scale of 1 to 10, how anxious were you?

Analyzing Emotions

After describing the experience, delve deeper into your emotions. What exactly did you feel? Was it fear, disgust, panic? Identifying your emotions helps you better understand your reaction and gradually defuse it.

Reflecting on Thoughts

Emotions are often accompanied by automatic thoughts like "Spiders are dangerous," "It's going to jump on me," etc. Note these thoughts. They are key to understanding how your mind transforms a neutral or slightly uncomfortable encounter into a terrifying experience.

Searching for Patterns

Over time, your journal will reveal patterns in your fears. Perhaps you'll discover that certain situations, times of day, or types of spiders trigger stronger reactions. This awareness is crucial for targeting your efforts to overcome fear.

Action and Reevaluation

The ultimate goal of this journal is not just to record your fears but to prompt you to take action. Use it to plan small exposures or challenges that you can undertake. After each attempt, jot down your thoughts and feelings. Over time, you will see your entries change, reflecting your evolution and your ability to manage the fear of spiders.

By keeping a fear journal, you engage in ongoing dialogue with yourself, exploring and dismantling the mechanisms of your arachnophobia. This process is not just a writing exercise; it's a quest for understanding, one step at a time, towards a life less hindered by fear.

Chapter 2: Understanding Strategic Brief Therapy

Basic Principles of the Palo Alto School

The Palo Alto School, pivotal in the fields of psychology and communication, revolutionized our understanding of human interactions and the treatment of psychological disorders. At the heart of this revolution is strategic brief therapy, an approach based on innovative principles. These principles shape a treatment method that is both concise and profoundly effective, especially in managing phobias such as arachnophobia.

Non-Verbal Communication and Metacommunication

One of the pillars of the Palo Alto School is the importance of non-verbal communication and metacommunication. The founders emphasized that what we say is only part of the equation; how we say it can often convey much more. This principle also applies to therapy, where the therapist observes and interacts with the client's communication patterns, including non-verbal messages and what they reveal about underlying issues.

The Problem is Not the Problem; the Solution is the Problem

This maxim, though enigmatic at first glance, summarizes the unique approach of strategic brief therapy. Often, repeated and unsuccessful attempts to solve a problem become a new problem themselves, creating a vicious cycle. In the case of arachnophobia, for example, avoiding spiders at all costs can reinforce the fear and make it more central in a person's life. Strategic brief therapy aims to break this cycle by changing how the client approaches the problem, rather than trying to directly solve the fear itself.

Solution-Oriented Approach Rather than digging into the past

to find the origins of a disorder, strategic brief therapy focuses on the present and the future. It aims to identify practical and achievable solutions that can be implemented immediately. This approach encourages the client to think differently, to experiment with new behaviors, and to observe the results, thus facilitating rapid and lasting change.

Paradoxical Tasks

Paradoxical interventions are another cornerstone of this approach. By asking the client to engage in behaviors that seem counterintuitive, the therapist can help disrupt problematic patterns. For someone with arachnophobia, this might mean, under supervision and in a very controlled manner, voluntarily interacting with spiders or images of spiders in order to defuse the automatic fear response.

Changing Perception

Strategic brief therapy works to alter the client's perception of their problem. By changing how a person views their interaction with spiders, it is possible to transform paralyzing fear into manageable apprehension, or even neutrality. This change in perception is crucial for allowing the client to regain control over their life, freed from the grip of the phobia.

Building on these fundamental principles, strategic brief therapy offers a powerful way to understand and overcome arachnophobia. By recognizing that the solutions attempted are often what perpetuate the problem, focusing on solution-oriented actions, employing paradoxical tasks, and aiming for a change in perception, this approach enables significant changes within a relatively short timeframe. For those looking to free themselves from the fear of spiders, understanding and applying the principles of the Palo Alto School can be an essential first step toward a more free and fulfilling life.

Application of Strategic Brief Therapy to Arachnophobia

Strategic brief therapy, with its roots deeply embedded in the innovative principles of the Palo Alto School, provides a powerful and flexible framework for addressing and transforming arachnophobia. This section explores how the fundamental principles of this approach can be specifically applied to help individuals navigate and overcome their fear of spiders.

Identifying and Breaking Problematic Cycles

The first step in applying strategic brief therapy to arachnophobia involves identifying the cycles of behavior and thought that perpetuate the phobia. Many individuals with a fear of spiders develop complex avoidance strategies, designed to protect them from confronting their fear. While this may offer temporary relief, it also reinforces the fear in the long term, creating a problematic cycle of fear and avoidance.

In collaboration with a therapist, the client learns to recognize these patterns and interrupt them. For example, instead of avoiding rooms or activities where an encounter with a spider is possible, the client may be encouraged to deliberately engage in these activities, but with new strategies in place to manage their fear response.

Use of Paradoxical Tasks

Paradoxical tasks are particularly effective in treating arachnophobia. These interventions may seem counterintuitive, but they aim to challenge and change the client's relationship with their fear. A paradoxical task might involve inviting the client to voluntarily increase their anxiety level in the presence of spiders in a controlled environment, thereby reversing the usual avoidance reflex.

This approach can help demystify fear, showing the client that anxiety can be tolerated and that their fear response does not have absolute control over their actions. Over time, this method leads to a reduction in the automatic fear response to spiders.

Changing Perception

A key element in the application of strategic brief therapy to arachnophobia is the work on perception. The therapist helps the client reconsider and recontextualize their fear of spiders, shifting from seeing it as an omnipresent threat to a manageable, or even neutral, aspect of their environment. This may involve challenging mistaken beliefs about spiders, such as the idea that they are all dangerous or aggressive, and replacing these beliefs with factual information and more nuanced perspectives.

Strengthening Resilience and Autonomy

Finally, strategic brief therapy aims to strengthen the client's resilience and autonomy in the face of their phobia. By developing anxiety management strategies and successfully experimenting with new behaviors, the client builds confidence in their ability to manage their fear. This leads to greater autonomy and a gradual decrease in the phobia, allowing the client to live with more freedom and fewer constraints imposed by arachnophobia.

By integrating these principles and techniques of strategic brief therapy, individuals with arachnophobia can find effective ways to understand, challenge, and ultimately transform their fear. This process not only promises a reduction in fear but also an opportunity for personal growth and development, paving the way for a life less restricted by fear and richer in possibilities.

Exercise: Identifying Unsuccessful Solution

Attempts One of the key concepts of strategic brief therapy is the idea that the solutions we try to apply to our problems can sometimes worsen or perpetuate them. In the case of arachnophobia, avoidance strategies or other behaviors meant to protect us from fear can actually reinforce it. This exercise guides you through the process of recognizing and questioning these unsuccessful solution attempts, thus paving the way for more effective approaches to managing your fear of spiders.

Step 1: Reflection and Identification

Begin by reflecting on all the strategies you have used so far to avoid or minimize your fear of spiders. LIst them without judgment. This could include behaviors such as avoiding certain rooms, asking someone else to check for spiders, or even changing your habits and activities to reduce the likelihood of encountering spiders.

Step 2: Effectiveness Assessment

For each listed strategy, evaluate its long-term effectiveness. Ask yourself: "Has this strategy decreased my fear of spiders or merely provided temporary relief?" "Has my fear increased or decreased since I started using this strategy?" Be honest in your assessment.

Step 3: Recognizing Consequences

Consider the consequences of these strategies on your daily life. Have they limited your activities or living space? Have they affected your relationships with others? By recognizing the costs of these solution attempts, you can begin to see how they might contribute to maintaining your fear rather than resolving it.

Step 4: Exploring Alternatives

Now that you've identified the unsuccessful strategies, it's time to think about alternatives. What other approaches could you try that might help you manage your fear in a more constructive way? Consider strategies that expose you to your fear in a gradual and controlled manner, or relaxation and anxiety management techniques that can help you remain calm in the presence of spiders.

Step 5: Planning and Action

Choose one or two alternatives that you are willing to try. Develop a simple action plan to integrate these new strategies into your life. Set achievable goals and start small. For example, if you decide to try gradual exposure, you might start by looking at pictures of spiders, then progress to videos, before attempting to approach a real spider in a controlled environment.

Step 6: Journaling and Reevaluation

Keep a journal of your experiences with these new strategies. Record your reactions, your progress, and any adjustments you think necessary to your approach. This will help you stay engaged in the process and recognize the progress made. Regularly reevaluate your strategies to ensure they are helping you move towards your goal of effectively managing your fear of spiders.

By taking the time to identify and question unsuccessful solution attempts, you open yourself up to new possibilities for confronting and reducing your arachnophobia. This process is not just a step towards overcoming your fear, but also an opportunity to learn and grow, equipping you with tools and strategies that can be applied to other life challenges.

Chapter 3: Preparing for Change Mentally

Preparing for Change Transitioning to a state of less fear and anxiety towards spiders, or any phobia, requires solid mental preparation. This preparation is crucial as it lays the foundation on which strategies for overcoming the phobia will be built and tested. Here's how you can mentally prepare for this journey towards change.

Cultivating a Growth Mindset

The first step in mental preparation for change is to cultivate a growth mindset. This means recognizing that your abilities to manage and overcome your fear are not fixed but can be developed with time, effort, and perseverance. Accept that the process will be gradual, with ups and downs, and that every experience, whether seen as a success or a failure, is an opportunity for learning.

Setting Realistic Goals

Setting clear and achievable goals is essential in preparing for change. These goals should be specific, measurable, attainable, relevant, and time-bound (SMART). Instead of aiming for a total absence of fear, which may be unrealistic in the short term, set goals to reduce your anxiety level towards spiders or to increase your ability to remain calm in their presence. These small goals will act as milestones on your path to overcoming arachnophobia.

Strengthening Intrinsic Motivation

Your motivation to change must come from within. Reflect on the personal reasons why you want to overcome your fear of spiders. Is it to improve your quality of life? To be able to engage in outdoor activities without anxiety? By identifying and reinforcing your intrinsic motivation, you create a powerful and lasting engine for change.

Practicing Mindfulness Mindfulness,

the art of being fully present and engaged with the current moment without judgment, can be a valuable tool in mental preparation for change. It helps you observe your thoughts and feelings of fear without attaching to them or amplifying them. Through regular practice of mindfulness, you can learn to treat spider-related anxiety as a temporary experience that you can observe and let pass, rather than as a permanent state to be avoided at all costs.

Visualizing Change

Visualization is a potent technique for preparing for change. It involves creating detailed mental images of yourself successfully handling situations involving spiders. Imagine staying calm and in control in the presence of a spider, or even observing it with curiosity rather than fear. This practice strengthens the neural pathways associated with these positive behaviors and attitudes, making their realization in reality easier.

Building Social Support

Change is often more achievable and sustainable when you have the support of those around you. Share your goals and aspirations with friends, family, or a support group that can offer encouragement and constructive feedback. Knowing you are not alone in this journey can greatly enhance your resilience and determination.

Preparing for Setbacks

Finally, an essential part of mental preparation for change is recognizing that the path will not always be linear. There may be moments of regression where your fear seems to surge back. Anticipating these moments and planning how to handle them can help you stay on course, even when the journey gets tough.

By embracing these mental preparation strategies, you not only equip yourself to face your fear of spiders but also embark on a journey of personal growth that extends well beyond the confines of this phobia.

Setting Clear and Achievable Goals

Transitioning to a life less dominated by arachnophobia requires a well-defined roadmap, marked by clear and achievable goals. This crucial step in your preparation for change forms the foundation of your journey towards overcoming your fear of spiders. Here's how to effectively set these goals.

Understanding Your Destination

Before you can chart a course, it's essential to know where you want to go. In the context of arachnophobia, this means understanding what "overcoming the fear of spiders" means to you. Is it being able to observe a spider without panicking? Being in the same room with a spider without feeling the need to flee? Or is it something more ambitious, like being able to move a spider outside your home without assistance? Clearly defining this success helps you to direct your efforts more targetedly.

Setting SMART Goals

SMART goals (Specific, Measurable, Achievable, Realistic, Time-bound) are particularly useful for structuring your journey. Applied to arachnophobia, they might look like this:

Specific: "I want to be able to look at a spider picture without feeling excessive anxiety."

Measurable: "I will measure my progress by noting my anxiety level on a scale of 1 to 10."

Achievable: "I will start with less intimidating spider images and progress to more realistic ones."

Realistic: "Given my current level of fear, achieving this goal in one month is realistic."

Time-bound: "I aim to reach this goal within four weeks."

Step by Step The temptation to aim for radical change can be strong, but small victories are often more enduring. Break down your goals into smaller, more manageable steps. For example, before you can look at a spider picture, you might first get accustomed to reading interesting facts about spiders to reduce fear and increase curiosity.

Flexibility and Readjustment

Be ready to adjust your goals based on your progress. If you find a goal too ambitious or not challenging enough, take the time to reevaluate it. This flexibility is crucial to maintaining your motivation and commitment to the process.

Celebrating Progress

Don't forget to recognize and celebrate each step you achieve towards your goal. Each small success builds your confidence and brings you closer to your ultimate goal. Whether it's managing to stay calm in front of a spider image or handling a real encounter without panicking, every progress deserves celebration.

By setting clear and achievable goals, you create a framework for your journey towards overcoming arachnophobia. This process not only encourages you to continue your progress but also ensures that each step forward is guided by thoughtful intention and a specific action plan.

Exercise: Positive Visualization of Coexisting with Spiders

Positive visualization is a powerful technique that can transform your approach to living with spiders by altering your perception of these often misunderstood creatures. This exercise guides you through a visualization process where you imagine living in harmony with spiders, thereby reducing the anxiety and fear they provoke.

Step 1: Preparation for Visualization

Find a quiet and comfortable place where you won't be disturbed. Sit or lie down in a relaxed position. Close your eyes and take a few deep breaths to help relax. Focus on relaxing every part of your body, from your feet to your head.

Step 2: Begin the Visualization

Imagine a place where you feel safe and happy. This can be a real or imagined place, such as a peaceful garden, a forest, or even your own living room. Visualize this place in as much detail as possible, using all your senses to make it come alive in your mind.

Step 3: Introduce Spiders into Your Visualization

Once you feel relaxed and at peace in this space, begin to integrate the idea of spiders into your visualization. First, imagine a small, distant, and non-threatening spider moving around your peaceful environment. Simply observe it going about its business without interfering or feeling fear.

Step 4: Modify Your Perception

Gradually change the way you perceive the spider in your visualization. Imagine that the spider contributes to the ecological balance of your safe place by eating insects and adding to the natural beauty of the space. Visualize yourself acknowledging its presence as a natural and beneficial part of the environment.

Step 5: Increase Interaction

When you feel comfortable with the spider's presence from a distance, begin to imagine closer interactions, still in your safe place. Visualize yourself observing the spider more closely, perhaps even allowing a small, harmless spider to walk on your hand, feeling no fear or disgust, only curiosity and a peaceful connection.

Step 6: Reinforce Positive Sensations

Focus on the positive sensations associated with this peaceful coexistence with spiders. Feel the freedom from fear, the pride of overcoming an old aversion, and the appreciation for the diversity of life.

Step 7: Conclusion of the Visualization

When you are ready, start to slowly return to your normal awareness. Thank yourself for the open-mindedness and courage you displayed during the exercise. Take a few deep breaths, stretch gently, and open your eyes when you feel ready.

Integration into Real Life

Regularly practice this visualization exercise to strengthen your new perception of spiders. Over time, you may find that your actual reactions to spiders in daily life start to mirror the positive feelings and harmonious cohabitation you've visualized.

This positive visualization exercise is not only a way to reduce fear of spiders; it's also a tool to cultivate inner peace and harmony with the natural world. By changing the way we view things, we can alter how we feel about them, opening the door to richer and more liberated life experiences.

Chapter 4: Confrontation Strategies

Techniques for Gradually Facing Your Fears

Facing your fears, especially of spiders, can seem daunting. However, by adopting a gradual approach, you can significantly reduce the intensity of your fear, step by step. Here are proven techniques to help you gradually confront your fears, thereby reducing the grip of arachnophobia on your life.

1. **Progressive Exposure:** Progressive exposure is a behavioral therapy technique that encourages you to confront your fear in a controlled and gradual manner. Start with situations that provoke low anxiety and slowly progress to more anxiety-inducing situations. For example, you might start by thinking about a spider, then progress to looking at pictures of spiders, followed by videos, and finally, try to approach a real spider In a safe environment

2. **Systematic Desensitization:** Similar to progressive exposure, systematic desensitization combines gradual exposure to the object of your fear with relaxation techniques. Before exposing yourself to a spider image, for example, you would practice deep breathing exercises or muscle relaxation. This process helps reduce the

fear response by associating states of relaxation with the object of fear.
3. **Visualization:** Before physically confronting your fear, visualization can be a valuable tool. Imagine yourself successfully facing your fears step by step. Visualize every detail of the experience, from your environment to your actions and emotional reactions, focusing on feelings of calm and control.

4. **Modeling:** Observing someone else successfully handle a spider can also help reduce your own fear. This can be done in person or through videos. Seeing someone else manage a situation that scares you calmly can decrease your anxiety and encourage you to adopt similar behavior.
5. **Virtual Reality Therapy (VR)** Virtual reality technology provides a safe, controlled method for exposure to spiders without real risk. VR allows you to experience the presence of spiders in a virtual setting, gradually increasing the level of realism and proximity based on your comfort level.
6. **Direct Confrontation** When you feel ready, directly confronting a spider in a controlled environment may be the final step in your exposure process. This should ideally be done with professional support, especially if your fear is severe. Start by observing a spider from a distance and gradually decrease this distance as you become more comfortable.

Integration into Daily Life

These techniques are not quick fixes but tools to gradually integrate into your everyday life. Each small victory over your fear should be acknowledged and celebrated. Remember, the goal is not to completely eliminate fear—a natural reaction—but to reduce its impact on your life, allowing you to live with more freedom and less anxiety.

By practicing these techniques to gradually confront your fears, you will build resilience and self-confidence that transcend your arachnophobia, opening the door to new experiences and an improved quality of life.

The Progressive Challenges Concept Inspired by Allen Carr

Drawing from Allen Carr's revolutionary method to quit smoking, which is based on understanding and altering addiction perceptions, we can adopt a similar strategy for tackling arachnophobia through "progressive challenges." This method aims to change the perception of the fear of spiders through a series of structured challenges, enabling gradual yet enduring changes in our relationship with these creatures.

Initial Understanding

Before beginning the challenges, it's crucial to understand why and how spiders induce fear. This involves analyzing common misconceptions about spiders, focusing on factual information that highlights their beneficial role in nature and minimal actual danger to humans.

Progressive Challenges

Designed to gradually desensitize the fear of spiders, each challenge moves from slightly worrying actions to more direct interactions:

Phase 1: Research and Education

Learn about spiders' ecological importance and harmless species.

Phase 2: Visual Exposure

Start with non-threatening spider images, progressing to more anxiety-inducing ones.

Phase 3: Virtual Interaction

Use virtual reality to safely interact with spiders.

Phase 4: Real Proximity

Visit places where you can observe spiders safely behind glass.

Phase 5: Direct Interaction

For those ready, possibly share a space with a spider or learn to safely relocate one.

Reevaluation and Reflection Reflect on each challenge: What did you learn? How has your view of spiders changed? This reflection is vital to reinforce positive shifts in your attitude towards spiders. Celebrate every progress step, much like Allen Carr suggests celebrating every success on the path to quitting smoking.

By embracing the concept of progressive challenges, you embark on a transformative journey, replacing fear with understanding and acceptance, not only to live without the paralyzing fear of spiders but also to enrich your life with a new perspective on the natural world.

Exercise: Creating Your Exposure Ladder

In overcoming arachnophobia, creating a personal exposure ladder is invaluable. This method lets you break down your confrontation with fear into manageable stages, each progressively exposing you to spiders until the fear subsides. Here's how to craft your exposure ladder, tailored to your needs and comfort level:

Fear Assessment Begin by evaluating your current fear level of spiders on a scale from 0 to 10, where 0 is no fear and 10 is extreme fear. This helps you gauge your starting point.

Step Identification Break your journey into clear, distinct stages. Each stage should slightly increase exposure compared to the previous one. For example:

Step 1 (Fear Level 1-2): Read interesting facts about spiders to build a positive knowledge base.

Step 2 (Fear Level 2-3): Watch drawings or non-threatening illustrations of spiders.

Step 3 (Fear Level 3-4): Observe photos of real spiders, starting with less intimidating species.

Step 4 (Fear Level 4-5): Watch videos of spiders in their natural environment.

Step 5 (Fear Level 5-6): Visit spider exhibitions at a

zoo or aquarium, where they are behind glass.

Step 6 (Fear Level 6-7): Observe a real spider from a distance in a controlled environment.

Step 7 (Fear Level 7-8): Gradually decrease the distance between you and a real spider, still in a controlled setting.

Step 8 (Fear Level 8-9): Learn to capture and release a spider using appropriate tools, such as a glass and a piece of paper.

3. Planning and Preparation

For each step, plan how you will approach it, which resources you will use (such as books, websites, videos), and in what kind of environment. Ensure you are in a receptive mindset and a place where you feel safe and in control.

4. Progress at Your Own Pace

Move through the exposure scale at your own pace. Only proceed to the next step when you feel comfortable with the current level of exposure. There is no rush; the goal is to sustainably improve your comfort with spiders, not to rush through the process.

5. Progress Journal
Keep a journal of your experiences at each stage of the exposure scale. Record your reactions, thoughts, and any changes in your level of fear. This journal can be a valuable source of reflection and motivation.

6. Adjustments if Necessary

Be prepared to adjust your exposure scale if needed. If a particular step proves too challenging, consider breaking it down into even smaller sub-steps. The important thing is to keep moving forward, no matter the pace.

By following these steps to create and use your exposure scale, you engage in a methodical and thoughtful process to confront and manage your fear of spiders. This process not only helps reduce your phobia but also strengthens your confidence and resilience in facing challenges.

Chapter 5: Modifying Internal Dialogue

Working on Thoughts and Beliefs About Spiders

Modifying internal dialogue, particularly regarding our thoughts and beliefs about spiders, is a crucial step in transforming arachnophobia. Our internal beliefs shape our reality, directly influencing our emotions and behaviors. By examining and adjusting these beliefs, we can change our perception of spiders, moving from fear to a more peaceful coexistence or even appreciation.

Identifying Negative Automatic Thoughts

The process begins by identifying the automatic thoughts that arise in the presence of spiders or at the thought of them. These thoughts are often irrational and exaggerated, such as "All spiders are dangerous" or "A spider will definitely bite me." Noting these thoughts as they appear helps you recognize and challenge them.

Questioning the Validity of Beliefs

Once you've identified your automatic thoughts, the next step is to question their validity. Ask yourself, "Are all spiders really dangerous?" "What are the actual chances of being bitten by a spider?" Look for facts and statistics that can challenge your beliefs. You'll often find that your fears are based on perceptions, not realities.

Reevaluating Beliefs

After confronting your automatic thoughts with facts, it's time to reevaluate your beliefs about spiders. Replace old beliefs with new, more nuanced ones based on reality. For example, instead of thinking all spiders are to be feared, recognize that most spiders are not dangerous to humans and play an essential role in the ecosystem.

Practicing Positive Thinking

Developing a positive internal dialogue about spiders can also help change your perception. Try practicing positive affirmations like, "I can learn to coexist with spiders" or "Spiders are fascinating creatures." By focusing on the positive aspects, you can begin to alter your emotional response.

Positive Visualization

Use visualization techniques to reinforce your new beliefs. Imagine encountering a spider and responding calmly, using your new beliefs to guide your response. Visualize controlling your fear with your renewed understanding of spiders.

Creating Corrective Experiences

Create corrective experiences by gradually exposing yourself to spiders in a controlled environment. Each positive interaction where your fears do not materialize helps refute old beliefs and reinforce new ones.

Changing Thoughts and Beliefs

Changing thoughts and beliefs about spiders requires time and practice but is crucial for altering your perception of these creatures. Actively working on your internal dialogue lets you control your phobia, leading to a life less restricted by fear and enriched with new experiences.

Using Cognitive Restructuring to Change Internal Dialogue

Cognitive restructuring, a cognitive-behavioral therapy technique, involves identifying, challenging, and changing negative automatic thoughts and unrealistic beliefs. This approach can be highly effective in transforming fear-dominated internal dialogue into a more rational and soothing self-exchange.

Identifying Distorted Thoughts

Become aware of specific automatic thoughts that arise in response to spider fears. These often include overgeneralizations, catastrophizing, or negative filtering.

Critical Questioning

Critically examine these thoughts by asking:

"What evidence do I have that this thought is true?"

"Is there another way to view the situation?"

"How would I react if a friend had this thought?"

This process helps assess the validity and utility of your automatic thoughts, confronting them with a less threatening reality.

Developing Counterarguments

To tackle identified negative thoughts, develop rational counterarguments. For instance, against the automatic thought "All spiders are dangerous," a counterargument might be "Most spiders are not harmful to humans, and encounters with dangerous spiders are extremely rare in my area."

Building New Thoughts

From these counterarguments, formulate new thoughts that are both realistic and supportive. These should reflect a more balanced and objective perspective on spiders and your ability to manage your fear. For example, "Even though I don't like spiders, I can learn safe ways to coexist with them."

Practice and Repetition

Cognitive restructuring requires practice and repetition. Actively integrate your new thoughts into your daily internal dialogue, especially in situations where you might encounter spiders or think about them. Over time, these new thoughts will become more automatic, lessening the impact of arachnophobia on your emotional well-being.

Evaluating Effectiveness

Regularly assess the effectiveness of this approach by noting changes in your anxiety levels and behavior around spiders or when thinking about them. Adjust your cognitive restructuring techniques as needed based on your progress and observations.

Cognitive restructuring provides a powerful way to change the internal dialogue about spiders, allowing you to replace fear and anxiety with greater understanding and acceptance. This internal work is crucial for living a life less restricted by arachnophobia, paving the way for new emotional freedom.

Exercise: Keeping a Thought Journal

Keeping a thought journal is a powerful exercise in cognitive restructuring, particularly effective for those looking to change their internal dialogue about spiders. This journal serves as a tool for awareness, helping you to identify, analyze, and modify the negative automatic thoughts that fuel arachnophobia. Here's how you can implement this exercise.

Setting Up the Journal Choose a notebook or a digital platform that is easily accessible and where you feel comfortable writing regularly. The format is less important than your commitment to using this tool consistently.

Recording Automatic Thoughts Whenever you catch yourself having a negative thought related to spiders, write it down in your journal. Be as specific as possible, describing the situation that triggered the thought, the thought itself, and the emotions felt. For example, "Seeing a spider in the living room, I thought: 'It will bite me, and I will become seriously ill.' I felt terrified."

Analysis of Thoughts

After recording an automatic thought, take a moment to analyze it. Ask yourself if this thought is realistic, what evidence supports its truth, and how you might view it differently. This process can be aided by the questioning techniques mentioned in cognitive restructuring.

Revision and Replacement

Next to each negative automatic thought, try to write a more realistic and kinder alternative thought. The goal is to find a more balanced way of viewing the situation that reduces your anxiety. For example, replace "It will bite me" with "Most spiders are harmless, and it is probably more scared of me than I am of it."

Monitoring and Reflection

Regularly use your journal to track your progress. Reflect on how your thoughts and feelings about spiders have changed over time. This will help you identify thought patterns you have successfully changed and areas where further work might be needed.

Sharing and Discussion

If comfortable, sharing entries from your journal with a therapist or support group can provide useful external perspectives and reinforce your cognitive restructuring process.

By maintaining a thought journal, you create a space to observe and modify your internal dialogue regarding spiders. This daily effort is a step towards a less anxious and more nuanced perception of spiders, gradually freeing you from the grip of arachnophobia in your life.

Chapter 6: Paradoxical Tasks

Introduction to Paradoxical Tasks in the Treatment of Arachnophobia

Paradoxical tasks offer a refreshing perspective on treating arachnophobia. These tasks may seem counterintuitive as they involve engaging in behaviors or thoughts that appear to contradict the immediate goal of reducing anxiety. However, their effectiveness lies in their ability to disrupt the usual cycles of fear and avoidance, paving the way for significant change in the individual's relationship with their phobia.

The Principle of Paradoxical Tasks

The foundation of paradoxical tasks is based on the notion that directly avoiding or combating a fear often reinforces it. For instance, in arachnophobia, continually avoiding spiders or scenarios where they might appear can intensify the fear and anxiety associated with these creatures. Paradoxical tasks invert this logic by proposing actions that counter the avoidance instinct, thus encouraging individuals to face their fears in a controlled and often unexpected manner.

Application to Arachnophobia

In the context of arachnophobia, paradoxical tasks are designed to destabilize the usual responses of fear and avoidance. Here are some examples:

- **Voluntarily Approaching Spiders**: Instead of avoiding areas where spiders may be present, individuals might be encouraged to actively explore these spaces, gradually increasing their tolerance to the presence of spiders.
- **Watching Spider Documentaries:** Encouraging someone who fears spiders to watch documentaries about them might seem counterintuitive. However, this visual immersion can help demystify spiders and reduce fear by providing factual information about their behavior and ecological role.
- **Imagining Scenarios Involving Spiders:** Asking a person to imagine not only neutral or positive interactions with spiders but also to consciously visualize their worst fears occurring without disastrous consequences can help to put things into perspective and reduce the emotional impact of these scenarios.

Effects of Paradoxical Tasks

Paradoxical tasks may initially seem to increase anxiety, which is a normal part of the process. However, persisting with these tasks often leads to a diminished emotional reaction to spiders. This effect is due to repeated exposure in a non-threatening context, allowing for a reevaluation and alteration of the perceived danger associated with spiders, leading to reduced fear.

The Importance of Professional Guidance

It is crucial that the implementation of paradoxical tasks, especially in the context of pronounced phobias like arachnophobia, be guided by a professional. A therapist can provide the necessary support to navigate through the emotional challenges these tasks may present, ensuring a safe progression tailored to the individual's pace.

Integrating paradoxical tasks in the treatment of arachnophobia adopts a strategy that not only encourages overcoming fear but also fosters a real transformation in how spiders are perceived and experienced. This aspect of therapy invites a deeper self-exploration, opening doors to new freedom and serenity from old fears.

How Paradoxical Tasks Help Break the Cycle of Fear

Paradoxical tasks, with their seemingly counterintuitive approach, play a crucial role in breaking the fear cycle associated with arachnophobia. They disrupt the usual patterns of thought and behavior that fuel and sustain the phobia. Here's how these unique tasks promote profound transformation in managing fear of spiders:

Direct Confrontation with Fear:

Paradoxical tasks encourage direct confrontation with the object of fear, in this case, spiders. This approach is fundamental to breaking the cycle of avoidance, which only strengthens fear in the long term. By voluntarily engaging in activities that induce anxiety, individuals learn to tolerate and manage their emotional reactions, gradually reducing the power that fear holds over them.

Reevaluation of Danger:

By directly interacting with spiders or exposing oneself to spider-related situations in a controlled manner, individuals are prompted to reassess the actual danger they pose. Paradoxical tasks provide a safe framework for this reevaluation, allowing people to discover firsthand that spiders are not as threatening as they believed. This process helps to dismantle the irrational beliefs fueling the phobia.

Modification of Conditioned Responses:

Fear of spiders is often a conditioned response—a reflexive reaction to the sight or thought of spiders. Paradoxical tasks, by exposing the individual to the object of their fear in a non-threatening way, help to modify these conditioned responses. Over time, the presence of a spider triggers less automatic anxiety, as repeated experiences teach the brain that these situations do not require an intense fear response.

Increase in Sense of Control:

A crucial aspect of fear is the feeling of losing control in the face of the dreaded situation. Paradoxical tasks return power to the individual by showing that they can choose how to interact with their fears. This regained control is vital for boosting self-confidence and reducing overall anxiety related to spiders.

Desensitization and Habituation:

Paradoxical tasks facilitate desensitization and habituation—processes by which repeated exposure to an anxiety-provoking stimulus gradually decreases the emotional response it elicits. By regularly and voluntarily confronting situations involving spiders, the individual becomes accustomed to their presence, and the initial fear reaction diminishes over time.

Catalyst for Reflection and Introspection:

Finally, paradoxical tasks act as a catalyst for deeper reflection and introspection about the nature of fear and personal anxiety management strategies. They encourage internal exploration, helping individuals understand the roots of their fear and develop healthier, more effective coping mechanisms.

By breaking the cycle of fear through paradoxical tasks, those with arachnophobia can experience significant changes, moving from constant avoidance and anxiety to a more peaceful coexistence with spiders. This path to emotional freedom is paved with experiences that defy expectations, revealing each individual's capacity to overcome their deepest fears.

EXERCICE : Designing Your Own Paradoxical Task

Creating your own paradoxical task is a powerful exercise for confronting and transforming your fear of spiders. The goal is to design an activity that seems to go against your instinct to avoid but actually helps you break the cycle of fear. Here's how you can develop this task step-by-step:

Initial Reflection Think about your fear of spiders and the avoidance behaviors you typically adopt. What situations do you avoid the most? What thoughts or beliefs support this fear? This initial reflection is crucial for identifying the specific area your paradoxical task should focus on.

Defining the Goal Set a clear, measurable goal for your paradoxical task. For example, "Reduce my anxiety level when a spider is in the same room," or "Be able to observe a spider without feeling the immediate need to flee."

Designing the Task Create a task that pushes you to directly confront the aspect of your fear of spiders you want to change. Ensure the task is achievable and makes you slightly uncomfortable, but not excessively so. For instance, if you usually avoid any images of spiders, your paradoxical task might be to look at a spider picture for one minute each day.

Planning and Preparation Plan how and when you will carry out your paradoxical task. Prepare everything you need to perform it under the best conditions. If your task involves looking at images of spiders, choose the images in advance. If it involves being in the same room as a spider, determine how you will secure the environment to feel in control.

Task Execution Carry out your paradoxical task as planned. Approach this experience with an open mind and a sense of curiosity. Observe your reactions without judgment and note any thoughts or feelings that arise.

Reflection and Adjustment

After completing your task, take time to reflect on the experience. How did you feel before, during, and after? Were there any surprises? How can you adjust the task to continue making progress? This reflection process is crucial for refining your approach and enhancing the benefits of the exercise.

Repetition and Expansion

Regularly repeat your paradoxical task, gradually increasing its intensity or difficulty. The goal is to continue pushing yourself out of your comfort zone at a manageable pace. Over time, you can expand the scope of your paradoxical tasks to include more varied and complex challenges.

By designing and implementing your own paradoxical task, you actively participate in your healing process. This exercise is not only a way to confront and reduce fear of spiders but also an opportunity to discover your resilience and ability to manage anxiety constructively.

Chapter 7: Strengthening Resilience

Techniques for Building Confidence and Resilience

Building resilience and self-confidence is crucial for overcoming arachnophobia or any deeply rooted fear. Resilience allows you to bounce back from anxiety-provoking situations, while self-confidence increases your ability to handle these situations effectively. Here are proven techniques to build these fundamental pillars.

Gradual and Controlled Exposure

One of the most effective methods for building confidence in your ability to handle fear of spiders is gradual exposure. Start with situations that cause mild anxiety and progress to more intimidating challenges. Each success strengthens your confidence and proves that you can handle anxiety constructively.

Mindfulness Practice

Mindfulness helps you stay grounded in the present moment, reducing anxiety caused by anticipatory thoughts or negative memories. Simple breathing techniques, guided meditation, or even daily mindful practices can enhance your ability to remain centered and calm, even in the presence of spiders.

Success Journal

Keeping a journal of your successes, big and small, in your fight against arachnophobia can be a powerful reminder of your ability to overcome challenges. Record each time you face your fear, and reflect on what these experiences teach you about your strength and resilience.

Positive Self-Talk

Changing how you talk to yourself can have a profound impact on your confidence and resilience. Replace negative thoughts and affirmations with positive and encouraging messages. For example, instead of thinking "I can't handle this", tell yourself "I am facing my fears and becoming stronger."

Setting Achievable Goals

Setting clear and achievable goals in your process of managing arachnophobia provides direction and a sense of progress. Celebrate each achieved goal as a victory, thus reinforcing your confidence in your ability to manage and overcome your fear.

Seeking Support Surrounding yourself with supportive and understanding people can significantly boost your resilience. Whether it's friends, family, or a support group, sharing your experiences and receiving encouragement can motivate you to keep moving forward.

Continuous Learning

Educating yourself about spiders and arachnophobia can transform fear of the unknown into rational understanding. Learning about the ecological role of spiders, for example, can lessen anxiety by altering your perception of these creatures.

Positive Visualization

Mentally reinforcing your confidence and ability to manage fear through positive visualization of successful encounters with spiders can be very effective. Imagine yourself handling a situation with a spider calmly, and feel the positive emotions associated with this success.

By integrating these techniques into your life, you build a strong foundation of self-confidence and resilience that will support you in your journey to overcome arachnophobia. These strategies not only equip you to handle spiders but also to manage other life challenges with greater assurance and improved resilience.

Importance of Mindfulness and Acceptance

In the journey to manage and overcome arachnophobia, mindfulness and acceptance play crucial roles. These concepts, while seemingly simple, offer profound depth and effectiveness in treating phobias and anxieties. They encourage an approach that not only helps manage fear of spiders but also promotes overall well-being.

Mindfulness: Living in the Present Moment

Mindfulness is the act of bringing one's complete attention to the present moment in an open, curious, and non-judgmental way. This practice teaches us to observe our thoughts, bodily sensations, and emotions without trying to change or avoid them. In the context of arachnophobia, this means welcoming thoughts and feelings of fear as they arise, recognizing them for what they are natural reactions to perceived threats and allowing them to pass without impulsively acting to eliminate them.

Acceptance: Embracing the Experience

Acceptance goes hand in hand with mindfulness and involves embracing the present experience without resistance. This doesn't mean resigning to or endorsing fear, but rather acknowledging that this fear exists at the moment. For those battling arachnophobia, practicing acceptance means acknowledging the fear of spiders without self-criticism or judgment, while understanding that this fear does not define who they are as a person.

The Role of Mindfulness and Acceptance in Managing Arachnophobia

Reducing Emotional Reactivity: Mindfulness creates a space between encountering a spider (or the thought of one) and our reaction. This space offers the opportunity to choose how to respond rather than automatically reacting with fear or aversion.

Developing Discomfort Tolerance: Acceptance encourages tolerating the discomfort that spiders may cause, recognizing that one can live with this sensation without it taking over their lives.

Decreasing Avoidance: By practicing mindfulness and acceptance, individuals are less likely to resort to avoidance behaviors, which, although reassuring in the short term, reinforce the phobia in the long term.

Increasing Self-Awareness: These practices lead to a better understanding of one's own reactions and motives, providing valuable insights that can be used to adjust fear management approaches.

Integration into Daily Life Integrating mindfulness and acceptance into daily life can start with small practices, such as taking a few minutes each day to meditate, practice mindful breathing, or simply observe without judgment one's own reactions to stressful situations. Over time, these practices can transform how you experience not only your phobia but also every aspect of your life.

By embracing mindfulness and acceptance, you equip yourself with powerful tools to navigate the world with greater serenity, a better understanding of yourself, and an enhanced ability to face challenges, including arachnophobia.

Exercise : Meditation and Mindfulness to Manage Anxiety

Meditation and mindfulness are powerful tools for managing anxiety, including that caused by arachnophobia. These techniques help to calm the mind, reduce stress, and increase self-awareness, enabling more effective management of emotional reactions. Here is a simple yet profound exercise to incorporate meditation and mindfulness into your daily routine to manage anxiety.

Meditation Preparation

Find a Quiet Space: Choose a place where you won't be disturbed during the exercise. This could be in your bedroom, a corner of your living room, or even outdoors if accessible.

Adopt a Comfortable Position: Sit on a chair with your feet flat on the floor, on a meditation cushion with your legs crossed, or even lie down if it's more comfortable for you. The important thing is to maintain a posture where your back remains straight yet relaxed.

Set an Intention: Before you start, take a moment to set an intention for your practice. This could be something like, "I am practicing mindfulness to welcome and soothe my anxiety."

Meditation Practice

Focus on Breathing: Gently close your eyes and start to focus on your breathing. Notice the air entering and leaving your nostrils, or your abdomen rising and falling with each breath. If your mind starts to wander, acknowledge it without judgment and gently bring your attention back to your breathing.

Observe Sensations: After a few minutes, expand your attention to include sensations throughout your body. Note areas of tension or relaxation without trying to change them. If you feel anxiety or fear when thinking about spiders, observe where this sensation resides in your body.

Welcome Emotions: Allow any present emotions, including anxiety, to manifest without trying to alter or avoid them. Practice acceptance of these emotions, recognizing them as transient experiences.

Using a Mantra or Affirmation: To help focus your mind, you can silently repeat a mantra or positive affirmation, such as "I am calm" or "I welcome my feelings with kindness."

Gentle Return: After 10 to 20 minutes, or when you feel ready, begin to bring your attention back to your environment. Slowly move your fingers and toes, stretch if necessary, and gently open your eyes.

Integration into Daily Life: The key to benefiting from meditation and mindfulness is regularity. Even a few minutes each day can significantly impact your anxiety management. Over time, this practice can help you develop a calmer, more receptive state of mind, reducing the impact of arachnophobia on your emotional well-being.

By learning to welcome and observe your thoughts and emotions without judgment through meditation and mindfulness, you build an inner space of calm and resilience, capable of facing anxiety and the fear of spiders with new strength and serenity.

Chapter 8: Living Without Fear

Integrating New Strategies into Everyday Life

After exploring various techniques and exercises to manage arachnophobia, the next crucial step is to integrate these new strategies into your daily life. This integration ensures that the progress made is not fleeting but becomes a lasting part of your response to spiders and anxiety in general. Here's how you can apply these strategies daily to maintain and enhance your resilience to fear.

Daily Practice of Mindfulness

Incorporate short sessions of mindfulness meditation into your daily routine. Start or end your day with a few minutes of mindful breathing or guided meditation. The goal is to cultivate a presence of mind that helps you manage anxiety proactively, rather than reacting impulsively to fear.

Applying Techniques of Gradual

Exposure Actively seek opportunities to practice gradual exposure in real-life situations. This might involve not immediately fleeing a room where a spider is present, or taking a moment to observe a spider from a distance, applying breathing techniques and mindfulness to manage your reaction.

Reflection and Journaling Continue

to keep a journal of your thoughts, emotions, and behaviors related to spiders and your phobia. Use this journal not only to track your progress but also to reflect on the strategies that work best for you. This allows you to adjust your approach based on your lived experiences.

Using Positive Affirmations

Create positive affirmations that resonate with you and repeat them regularly. For example, "I am capable of managing my fear of spiders" or "Every day, I become calmer and more confident." These affirmations can serve as powerful reminders of your ability to overcome anxiety.

Strengthening Support Networks

Share your experiences and progress with friends, family, or support groups who can offer encouragement and understanding. Social support is a key pillar in maintaining motivation and reinforcing fear management strategies.

Integration into Daily Activities

Find ways to incorporate exposure and anxiety management strategies into your daily activities. For example, if reading about spiders helps demystify them, include this practice in your morning reading routine.

Celebrating Success

Recognize and celebrate every victory, big or small, on your path to managing arachnophobia. These celebrations reinforce a sense of achievement and motivate continued application of learned strategies.

Integrating new strategies into daily life is a dynamic process that requires attention and commitment. By regularly applying these strategies, you build a solid foundation for a life less limited by fear, where spiders no longer define your boundaries. This journey towards emotional freedom and serenity is enriched by every small step you take each day.

How to Maintain Long-Term Progress After working on your fears and integrating new strategies for managing arachnophobia, the challenge is to maintain these advancements long-term. The permanence of your transformation depends on continuous practices and mindful vigilance. Here are tips to ensure that the progress you've made in your relationship with spiders and anxiety management remains strong and enduring.

Regular Practice

The key to maintaining your progress is regularity. Whether it's mindfulness exercises, visualization sessions, or controlled exposure to spiders, integrating these practices into your daily or weekly routine is essential. Consider these activities as an integral part of your lifestyle, just like physical exercise or a healthy diet.

Setting New Goals

As time progresses, your initial goals for managing arachnophobia might need updates. Set new challenges that reflect your current comfort level and confidence with spiders, keeping you motivated and engaged in your personal journey.

Gratitude and Progress Journal

Maintaining a journal of gratitude and progress can powerfully document and celebrate your achievements. Record moments of successful fear management, newly integrated strategies, and everyday victories. Reviewing these entries can boost your motivation and resilience on challenging days.

Social Support

Support from family, friends, or support groups is crucial in maintaining progress. Share your experiences and successes with them to reinforce your commitment and inspire others in their own challenges.

Ongoing Education

Continue educating yourself about spiders and anxiety management techniques. Ongoing learning can provide new insights and strategies for confronting fears, enhancing your understanding and appreciation of spiders, which naturally reduces fear.

Self-Compassion and Patience

Recognize that maintaining progress is a journey with ups and downs. Practice patience and kindness towards yourself during setbacks. Self-compassion is vital to navigate these moments without losing sight of the progress made.

Reevaluation and Adjustment

Regularly take time to reassess your strategies and progress. Being open to adjusting your methods ensures they remain aligned with your current needs and goals, keeping your approach effective and relevant.

Adopt a Long-Term Perspective

Finally, embrace a long-term perspective on your journey to live without fear. Recognizing that maintaining progress is a lifelong commitment will help you stay dedicated to practices that support your well-being.

By incorporating these strategies into your life, you solidify the necessary foundations to maintain your progress against arachnophobia. In doing so, you not only sustain the changes you've achieved but also continue to grow and evolve in your ability to manage anxiety and live a fully fulfilled life.

Exercise: Creating a Personalized Maintenance Plan

To ensure long-term success in managing arachnophobia or any other fear, it's crucial to develop a personalized maintenance plan. This plan helps you stay focused, motivated, and prepared for future challenges. Here's how you can create your own maintenance plan:

Assessment and Reflection: Begin by honestly evaluating your progress. Identify which strategies have been effective and where challenges persist. Reflect on your journey, acknowledging obstacles overcome and resources that helped.

Setting Ongoing Goals: Based on your assessment, set clear, realistic, and measurable goals to continue managing your fear.

Maintenance Strategies: List specific strategies you will use to maintain progress, such as regular mindfulness practice, scheduled exposure sessions, visualization exercises, and participating in support groups.

Planning Regular Reviews: Incorporate regular reviews of your goals and strategies into your plan. These could be monthly, quarterly, or semi-annually.

Maintenance Journal: Keep a journal dedicated to

your maintenance plan. Record goals, strategies, successes, and challenges. This journal will serve as a reminder of your achievements and a guide during reviews.

Support Network: Identify supportive individuals or professionals who can help sustain your progress. Having a support network can provide strength during tough times.

Contingency Plan for Difficult Times: Prepare specific strategies for potential challenges. Include techniques like deep breathing, reminders of past successes, or comforting activities.

Celebrating Success: Ensure your plan includes ways to celebrate your successes, both big and small. Celebrating achievements can boost motivation and commitment to long-term well-being.

By creating and following a personalized maintenance plan, you equip yourself to sustain the progress made in managing your arachnophobia, leading to a more peaceful and fulfilling life.

Conclusion

Reflections on the Journey to Freedom from Spider Fear

Throughout this detailed journey, we've explored various strategies and exercises designed to help you manage and potentially overcome arachnophobia. This journey is personal and unique for everyone, yet it follows a common thread: transforming fear into understanding, acceptance, and eventually freedom.

Review of the Path Taken We began by recognizing and identifying specific fears related to spiders, a crucial step in understanding the origins of your anxiety. We then introduced innovative approaches such as brief strategic therapy and Allen Carr's method, which pave the way for confronting and deconstructing these fears.

Exposure Strategies and Inner Dialogue Modification Techniques like gradual exposure and mindfulness practice have been emphasized as powerful means to decrease sensitivity to spider-induced anxiety. Concurrently, cognitive restructuring work has profoundly changed internal dialogues, replacing fear and aversion with a more neutral or even positive outlook.

Paradoxical Challenges and Resilience Building

The use of paradoxical tasks demonstrated how engaging in seemingly counterintuitive actions can effectively break the cycle of fear. Additionally, building confidence and resilience has been crucial in supporting this change process, providing tools to manage anxiety and promote ongoing personal growth.

Integration and Maintenance The final part of this journey highlighted the importance of integrating new strategies into daily life and creating a personalized maintenance plan to ensure the sustainability of the progress made. Reflecting on these techniques helps consolidate the changes and prepares you for a life with less fear and more fulfillment.

Toward Renewed Freedom:

This journey to freedom from spiders is not just a set of steps to follow; it's a commitment to living a life less constrained by fear. Each strategy, exercise, and reflection contributes to a broader set of life skills that not only help you manage arachnophobia but also equip you to face other challenges with courage and resilience.

Looking back, it's clear that the real journey is not just about living without fear of spiders, but about discovering your inner strength and turning obstacles into opportunities for growth. The path to freedom from spiders is paved with learning, understanding, and acceptance a path that leads to a richer, more fulfilling life.

Encouragements for Continuing Your Journey:

As you continue on the path to freedom from arachnophobia, it's important to recognize the bravery, resilience, and dedication you have shown so far. Every small step you have taken is proof of your inner strength and ability to overcome obstacles. Here are some words of encouragement to support you on your continuing journey.

Celebrate Each Victory:

Always take time to celebrate every bit of progress. Recognizing each step you take in facing your fears or implementing new strategies helps to fuel your motivation and strengthens your commitment to personal growth.

Be Patient and Kind to Yourself: The journey to overcoming arachnophobia includes ups and downs. Be patient and compassionate with yourself during moments of doubt or frustration. Personal growth takes time, and every experience contributes to your learning.

Stay Open and Curious: Embrace new strategies and perspectives that can enrich your journey. Curiosity drives change, urging you to explore new ways of thinking and acting that can alter your relationship with spiders and your anxiety.

Seek Support: You're not alone in this journey. Seek out therapists, support groups, or others who have faced similar challenges. Sharing experiences and strategies can provide comfort and new ideas for moving forward.

Consider the Journey a Source of Enrichment:

Remember, the goal isn't just to live without fear of spiders but to grow and thrive through this challenge. Each effort you make strengthens you for other life challenges.

Look Forward with Hope:

Face the future with hope and confidence in your ongoing progress. Each new day is an opportunity to build on what you've achieved and to discover new freedoms.

Keep moving forward with courage and confidence, knowing each step you take is a testament to your resilience and your desire to live a fuller, richer life free from the grip of arachnophobia. Your journey is inspirational, and each new step holds infinite possibilities. Continue with the assurance that you have everything within you to move towards a fulfilling future.

Made in the USA
Columbia, SC
02 December 2024